EXPLORING COUNTRIES

# Belgium

by Lisa Owings

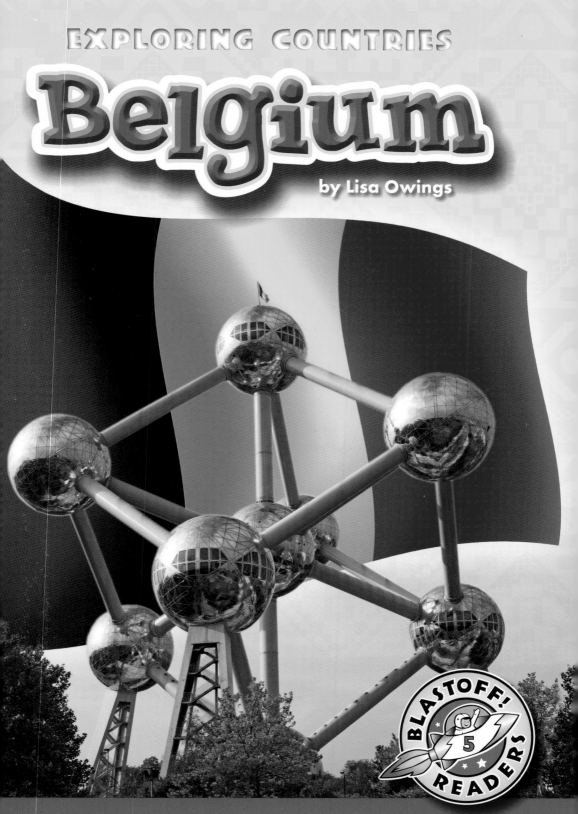

BELLWETHER MEDIA • MINNEAPOLIS, MN

Note to Librarians, Teachers, and Parents:

**Blastoff! Readers** are carefully developed by literacy experts and combine standards-based content with developmentally appropriate text.

**Level 1** provides the most support through repetition of high-frequency words, light text, predictable sentence patterns, and strong visual support.

**Level 2** offers early readers a bit more challenge through varied simple sentences, increased text load, and less repetition of high-frequency words.

**Level 3** advances early-fluent readers toward fluency through increased text and concept load, less reliance on visuals, longer sentences, and more literary language.

**Level 4** builds reading stamina by providing more text per page, increased use of punctuation, greater variation in sentence patterns, and increasingly challenging vocabulary.

**Level 5** encourages children to move from "learning to read" to "reading to learn" by providing even more text, varied writing styles, and less familiar topics.

Whichever book is right for your reader, Blastoff! Readers are the perfect books to build confidence and encourage a love of reading that will last a lifetime!

This edition first published in 2013 by Bellwether Media, Inc.

No part of this publication may be reproduced in whole or in part without written permission of the publisher. For information regarding permission, write to Bellwether Media, Inc., Attention: Permissions Department, 5357 Penn Avenue South, Minneapolis, MN 55419.

Library of Congress Cataloging-in-Publication Data
Owings, Lisa.
  Belgium / by Lisa Owings.
    p. cm. – (Blastoff! readers: exploring countries)
  Includes bibliographical references and index.
  Summary: "Developed by literacy experts for students in grades three through seven, this book introduces young readers to the geography and culture of Belgium"–Provided by publisher.
  ISBN 978-1-60014-761-6 (hardcover : alk. paper)
  1. Belgium–Juvenile literature.  I. Title.
DH418.O95 2013
949.3–dc23                           2012002388

Printed in the United States of America, North Mankato, MN.

# Contents

Where Is Belgium?          4

The Land                   6

Karst and Caves            8

Wildlife                  10

The People                12

Daily Life                14

Going to School           16

Working                   18

Playing                   20

Food                      22

Holidays                  24

Comic Strip Art           26

Fast Facts                28

Glossary                  30

To Learn More             31

Index                     32

# Where Is Belgium?

Netherlands

North Sea

English Channel

Brussels ★

Belgium

France

N
W   E
S

**Did you know?**

Belgium is divided into three main regions. The southern half is called Wallonia, and the northern half is Flanders. The small Brussels-Capital Region lies in the center of Belgium.

Germany

Luxembourg

Belgium is a small country in northwestern Europe. It covers only 11,787 square miles (30,528 square kilometers). France borders Belgium to the southwest. Germany and Luxembourg are its neighbors to the east, and the Netherlands lies to the north. Belgium's northwestern coast touches the North Sea. Across the English **Channel** is the United Kingdom.

Belgium's central location makes it an ideal global meeting place. Organizations such as the **European Union** and the **North Atlantic Treaty Organization** meet in the country's capital, Brussels.

## fun fact

With around 3,000 castles, Belgium has more per square mile than any other country in the world.

The Belgian landscape is mostly flat with some gentle hills in the south. The coastline features grass-covered **dunes** and sandy beaches. **Lowlands** stretch from the sea to the Schelde River. This river flows northeast through western Belgium. The wooded Kempenland region in the northeast is full of meadows and marshes.

The Central **Plateaus** are bordered by the Schelde River in the north and the Meuse River in the south. This region of rolling green hills has plenty of rich farmland. Most of Belgium's largest cities lie in this area. In the southeast, the land slopes into the forested hills of the Ardennes region.

Just south of the Meuse River, the Condroz region is defined by unique **limestone** rock formations. Over time, slightly **acidic** water breaks down some of the limestone. The resulting terrain is called a karst landscape. The most spectacular features of Belgium's karst landscape are caves.

The Grottes de Han near Han-sur-Lesse are some of the most fascinating caves in Europe. **Stalactites** drip like icicles from limestone ceilings. **Stalagmites** rise from the cave floor. Thin rock formations that look like curtains hang above underground rivers and lakes. Visitors come from near and far to admire the beauty of Belgium's caves.

## Did you know?

Many adventurous Belgians enjoy a sport called caving. They use ropes and other safety equipment to help them crawl, climb, and even swim through caves.

sandpiper

European
hedgehog

lily of
the
valley

## fun fact
Lily of the valley is a fragrant
flower that blooms all over
Belgium. It is common for Belgians
to give bunches of these flowers to
loved ones on the first day of May.

People have crowded out much of Belgium's wildlife.
However, the country is still home to many familiar
animals. Wild boars, wildcats, and red foxes roam the
forests of the Ardennes. Eagle owls fly silently overhead.
Wolves, bison, and wild horses can still be seen in the
wildlife reserve at Han-sur-Lesse.

eagle owl

The land north of the Ardennes is home to many smaller animals. Rabbits, muskrats, and hamsters scurry across the plateau. European hedgehogs find shelter in the east. Storks, geese, and sandpipers strut along the coast. Whales and gray seals sometimes swim close to shore.

## Did you know?

Around 70,000 German-speaking people live near Belgium's border with Germany. German is Belgium's third official language after Dutch and French.

Belgium is home to over 10 million people. About six out of every ten Belgians live in Flanders and speak Dutch. About three out of every ten Belgians speak French in Wallonia. Flemings and Walloons generally get along as fellow Belgians. However, some want the country to be divided into two independent nations.

About one out of every ten Belgians comes from Africa, Asia, or elsewhere in Europe. Belgium is home to people from France, Italy, and Germany. Turkish and Kurdish **immigrants** have settled in larger cities. Some Belgians also come from Morocco and other African countries.

## Speak Dutch!

| English | Dutch | How to say it |
| --- | --- | --- |
| hello | hallo | HAH-loh |
| good-bye | tot ziens | TOTE ZEENS |
| yes | ja | yah |
| no | nee | nay |
| please | alstublieft | AHLS-too-bleeft |
| thank you | dank u | DAHNGK oo |
| friend (male) | vriend | vreent |
| friend (female) | vriendin | vrihn-DIHN |

Nearly all Belgians live in cities. Adults usually drive cars or take the train to work. Children take the bus or ride their bikes to school. Most families live in modern houses. Belgians take pride in their homes, but they also like their privacy. They tend to only invite family and close friends inside.

Belgians pay high **taxes** for a high quality of life. The country has excellent health care and little **poverty**. It also has one of the largest railroad systems in the world. Newspapers, television shows, and other media are offered in multiple languages so all Belgians can stay informed.

## fun fact

A high-speed rail network links Brussels to cities in France, Germany, and the Netherlands. Passengers zip between these countries on trains that travel over 180 miles (290 kilometers) per hour!

# Where People Live in Belgium

countryside
3%

cities
97%

Most Belgian children start preschool around 3 years old. Primary school begins at age 6. Students learn math, science, social studies, and other subjects. Classes are taught in French, Dutch, or German. Learning a second or third language is important for Belgian students. It helps them communicate with others in Belgium and **abroad**.

After six years of primary school, Belgian students move on to six years of secondary school. Some secondary schools prepare students for college. Others train them in business, the arts, or various **trades**. Those who complete secondary school can attend one of Belgium's universities.

## Where People Work in Belgium

manufacturing 25%

services 73%

farming 2%

Most Belgians have **service jobs** in cities. Many work for the government. Others have jobs in schools, hospitals, and banks. Some Belgians make steel and **textiles** to sell to other countries. Factories in Antwerp produce fuel and cut diamonds.

In the countryside, workers dig chalk, limestone, and sand from the earth. These materials are made into cement and glass. A few farmers raise pigs or cattle for meat and dairy products. Others grow potatoes, sugar beets, grains, or fruits. Fishers bring in small catches of fish and **mussels** from the North Sea.

**Did you know?**

Belgian cycling champion Eddy Merckx is one of the country's heroes. He won the Tour de France every year between 1969 and 1972. He won it for the fifth time in 1974.

Belgians spend much of their free time outdoors. Cycling is one of the most popular sports. The country has hundreds of miles of bike paths. Belgians also enjoy soccer and car racing. Pigeon racing is an unusual but exciting sport. Trained pigeons are timed to see which one can fly home the fastest.

The Ardennes region is great for hiking, canoeing, and hunting. Belgians head to the sea to swim or relax in the sand and sun. In the city, people can visit one of Belgium's many art museums or attend a concert.

## fun fact

People come to the Belgian town of Spa to bathe and relax. Its waters are believed to have healing qualities. This is where the English word *spa* comes from.

Belgian waffles

Belgium is known for its delicious food. Thousands of restaurants and cafés serve meals featuring beef, pork, chicken, and seafood. *Waterzooi* is a **traditional** chicken or fish stew. *Moules frites* is one of the country's most popular dishes. Bowls of mussels are served with fries on the side.

Belgian waffles are made fresh while customers watch. They are sprinkled with powdered sugar and served hot. Many waffle stands offer additional toppings of fruit, chocolate sauce, and whipped cream. Belgium is also known for its chocolates. Rich truffles, fancy pralines, and other fine Belgian chocolates are famous around the world.

## fun fact

Belgians insist that fries were invented in Belgium, not France. Belgian *frites* are fried twice to make them extra crispy.

Belgian chocolates

moules frites

## Did you know?

The Festival of Cats is held every third summer in Ypres. Long ago, unwanted cats were thrown from the city's bell tower. This festival celebrates cats with cat costumes and a parade of giant cats.

Belgian celebrations are both odd and fun. People flock to Binche for a carnival in the days leading up to **Lent**. Performers called Gilles wear masks with glasses and mustaches. They throw oranges into the crowd as they pass by.

Fireworks light up the night sky on July 21, Belgium's Independence Day. Each August, giant figures from Belgian **folklore** parade through the streets of Ath. In December, Christmas markets transform cities such as Brussels into magical places. People gather to enjoy the lights, traditional foods, and winter fun.

Gilles

**Tintin and Snowy**

Belgium has a long history of art and invention. Comic strip art emerged from this tradition. The most famous Belgian comic features a teenage reporter named Tintin and his dog, Snowy.

Smurfs

The Smurfs are also a Belgian creation. These silly blue creatures have become popular throughout the world. Other well-known Belgian comic strips in both French and Dutch include *Lucky Luke*, *Suske en Wiske*, and *Le Chat*. Comic strip art exhibits the Belgian spirit of creativity and humor.

# Fast Facts About Belgium

## Belgium's Flag

The Belgian flag has three vertical stripes of black, yellow, and red. The colors come from the Belgian coat of arms, which features a yellow lion with red claws against a black background. The Belgian flag was first flown in the 1830s.

**Official Name:** Kingdom of Belgium

**Area:** 11,787 square miles (30,528 square kilometers); Belgium is the 141st largest country in the world.

| | |
|---|---|
| **Capital City:** | Brussels |
| **Important Cities:** | Antwerp, Ghent, Charleroi, Liège |
| **Population:** | 10,438,353 (July 2012) |
| **Official Languages:** | Dutch, French, German |
| **National Holiday:** | Independence Day (July 21) |
| **Religions:** | Roman Catholic (75%), Other (25%) |
| **Major Industries:** | farming, manufacturing, services, tourism |
| **Natural Resources:** | stone, sand, chalk, limestone |
| **Manufactured Products:** | steel, automobiles, diamonds, chemicals, textiles, glass, fuel, food products |
| **Farm Products:** | beef, pork, dairy products, potatoes, sugar beets, grains, fruits |
| **Unit of Money:** | Euro; the euro is divided into 100 cents. |

# Glossary

**abroad**—outside of one's home country

**acidic**—containing acid; acidic materials can dissolve rock and other minerals.

**channel**—a narrow waterway that separates two countries

**dunes**—hills of sand formed by wind or water

**European Union**—a group of European countries with many shared laws and rights

**folklore**—stories, customs, and beliefs that are handed down from one generation to the next

**immigrants**—people who leave one country to live in another country

**Lent**—the forty weekdays before the Christian holiday of Easter

**limestone**—a stone used in construction; limestone is formed over millions of years from old coral and shells.

**lowlands**—areas of land that are lower than surrounding land

**mussels**—shellfish that look similar to clams but have dark shells

**North Atlantic Treaty Organization**—a group of countries that have agreed to give one another military support

**plateaus**—areas of flat, raised land

**poverty**—lack of money

**service jobs**—jobs that perform tasks for people or businesses

**stalactites**—icicle-shaped formations that hang from the roofs of caves

**stalagmites**—cone-shaped formations that stick up from the floors of caves

**taxes**—money collected from people and businesses by the government; taxes support government programs.

**textiles**—fabrics or clothes that have been woven or knitted

**trades**—specific jobs or crafts

**traditional**—relating to stories, beliefs, or ways of life that families or groups hand down from one generation to the next

# To Learn More

## AT THE LIBRARY

Hergé. *The Adventures of Tintin: The Shooting Star.* Trans. Leslie Lonsdale-Cooper and Michael Turner. Boston, Mass.: Little, Brown, 1978.

Lamont, Gretchen. *The Mail-Carrier Cats of Liège.* Bloomington, Ind.: iUniverse, 2007.

Pateman, Robert, and Mark Elliot. *Belgium.* New York, N.Y.: Marshall Cavendish Benchmark, 2006.

## ON THE WEB

Learning more about Belgium is as easy as 1, 2, 3.

1. Go to www.factsurfer.com.

2. Enter "Belgium" into the search box.

3. Click the "Surf" button and you will see a list of related Web sites.

With factsurfer.com, finding more information is just a click away.

# Index

activities, 20-21
Antwerp, 19
Ardennes, 7, 10, 11, 21
Ath, 25
Binche, 25
Bruges, 19
Brussels, 4, 5, 14, 19, 25, 27
Brussels-Capital Region, 4
capital (see Brussels)
castles, 6
comic strip art, 26-27
daily life, 14-15
education, 16-17
European Union, 5
Festival of Cats, 24
Flanders, 4, 13
food, 22-23
holidays, 24-25
housing, 14
immigration, 13
Independence Day, 25
karst and caves, 8-9
landscape, 6-9
languages, 12, 13, 14, 16, 27
Lent, 25
location, 4-5
Merckx, Eddy, 20
Meuse River, 7, 8
North Atlantic Treaty
    Organization, 5

people, 12-13
Schelde River, 6, 7
Spa, 21
sports, 9, 20
transportation, 14
Wallonia, 4, 13
wildlife, 10-11
working, 18-19
Ypres, 24